BRITAIN IN OLD PHOTOGRAPHS

SOUTHWARK, BERMONDSEY AND ROTHERHITHE

STEPHEN HUMPHREY

ALAN SUTTON PUBLISHING LIMITED

Alan Sutton Publishing Limited
Phoenix Mill · Far Thrupp · Stroud
Gloucestershire · GL5 2BU

First published 1995
Reprinted 1996
Copyright © Stephen Humphrey, 1995

Cover illustration: Fogden's, decorated for the
carnival of July 1900 (see page 123).

Title-page illustration: Wigan & Co.'s hop
warehouses, seen from Calvert's Buildings,
Southwark. Hop warehouses were once
numerous in the area. The jettied building to
the right is one of the oldest buildings of the
district: 16th- or 17th-century.

British Library Cataloguing in Publication Data.
A catalogue record for this book is available from
the British Library.

ISBN 0-7509-0775-4

Typeset in 9/10 Sabon.
Typesetting and origination by
Alan Sutton Publishing Limited.
Printed in Great Britain by
Ebenezer Baylis, Worcester.

Acknowledgement is gladly made to the Guildhall Library, Corporation
of London, for the use of the view of the Marshalsea Prison on page 19;
to Mr C. Rumbold for the photograph of Abbey Buildings on page 81; to
Mrs J. Warren for the picture of Monarch Buildings on page 71; and to
Charterhouse-in-Southwark for the photographs of the Long Lane area
on pages 21 and 22. The rest of the photographs belong to the Southwark
Local Studies Library, and are used by kind permission of the Local
Studies Librarian, Mrs Janice Brooker.

Contents

Worsdale Cottages, off Newington Causeway, 1924.

Introduction

The mediaeval town of Southwark began as a pre-Conquest *burh* or fortified town, which was built to defend a river-crossing to the walled City of London opposite. Until as late as 1750 what we now call Old London Bridge was the only bridge across the Thames in London. The approach to that bridge on the Southwark side – Borough High Street – was therefore a major route for travellers and became noted for its coaching inns. They survived until after the coming of the railways and long enough to appear in a number of Dickens's novels. The local symbol of the new order, London Bridge Station, was the terminus of London's first railway in 1836.

All the districts covered by this book constituted the north-east corner of the historic county of Surrey. Indeed, Southwark was for long the largest and most populous town in the county and formed, in conjunction with Bermondsey and Rotherhithe, by far the most important industrial area of Surrey. Bermondsey and Rotherhithe were separate parishes with their own administrations down to 1900; Southwark was divided into no fewer than six parishes and three manorial jurisdictions. Of these, St. Saviour's Parish was the most important, and the parish of St. George the Martyr to its south covered the largest area. Christ Church Parish in the vicinity of Blackfriars Road, which was co-extensive with the manor of Paris Garden, was a backwater by comparison.

For many centuries the great church of St. Saviour was the dominating building in Southwark. It had served an Augustinian priory in the Middle Ages, and was allowed to become a parish church under King Henry VIII. Its parish was populous and busy. It was there that the Bishops of Winchester had a large town house until the 17th century and there that William Shakespeare's Globe Theatre stood from 1599 to 1644. His brother, Edmund, was buried in St. Saviour's in 1607, the same year in which John Harvard was baptized in the church. Harvard briefly owned an inn in Borough High Street before selling it to endow his college in Massachusetts. St. Saviour's was partly rebuilt in the 19th century and was lucky to escape demolition at the hands of the railways. In 1905 it was made the cathedral church of a new Diocese of Southwark and survives proudly today, a link with the very earliest discernible phase of Southwark's history.

The waterfronts of Southwark, Bermondsey and Rotherhithe became busy parts of the expanding Port of London in the 18th and 19th centuries. Rotherhithe had once been noted for shipbuilding and retained facilities for ship-repairing until quite recently. From the early 19th century the Surrey Commercial

Docks grew to encompass a major part of the peninsula between the Lower Pool and Limehouse Reach. By 1914 the system comprised nine wet docks, six timber ponds and a canal three and a half miles long which reached Camberwell and Peckham. Everywhere along the waterfront there were wharves, attracting shoals of barges as well as sea-going ships. In Rotherhithe the dominant trade was in timber. In Bermondsey foodstuffs were very important, giving rise to numerous food-processing factories. Bryan Donkin's factory in Southwark Park Road was the first to produce canned food. These food factories stood alongside the more ancient leather tanneries, which are given their own section in this book. Farther west, in Southwark, the predominant industries were beer and vinegar brewing, engineering, hat making and the trade in hops. The great engineering practice of John Rennie and his son was based in Southwark, and in Rotherhithe at about the same time Sir Marc Brunel and his son, Isambard Kingdom Brunel, built the first underwater tunnel in the world.

The first bridge to break Old London Bridge's monopoly was Westminster Bridge (1750). Its building prompted the layout of Westminster Bridge Road and New Kent Road. The opening of Blackfriars Bridge (1769) then led to the very grand scheme which comprised Blackfriars Road, St. George's Circus, Borough Road and London Road. Waterloo Bridge (1817) and Southwark Bridge (1819) – Dickens's 'Iron Bridge' – followed. The approach roads to all these bridges were like the spokes of a wheel, which converged on the junction known as the Elephant and Castle. As a result, that junction became one of the busiest in South London. It had long been a lesser junction between the old Roman route from London to Chichester and a local route from the Old Kent Road to Lambeth. Its transformation after 1750 led to successive rebuildings of the public house which gave the place its name until the building towered over the junction. The late Victorian version of the Elephant and Castle Public House was demolished in 1959 as part of the London County Council's megalomaniac scheme to 'redevelop' the area. It is undoubtedly the case that postwar clearances destroyed more historic buildings (and the vitality of districts) than wartime bombing. Nelson Square off Blackfriars Road, the Old Kent Road Library and countless Georgian buildings in the vicinity of the Bricklayers' Arms junction, Mayflower Street in Rotherhithe and waterfront houses in Rotherhithe Street were among the more important victims of postwar destruction.

The district of Walworth, south of the Elephant and Castle, differed from Southwark, Bermondsey and Rotherhithe in being largely residential and not noted for industry. It was bordered by Kennington Park Road on the one side and by the Old Kent Road on the other, with Walworth Road running through the centre and acting as its high street. The area had been rural until the 18th century, when the building of new bridges led to its becoming a genteel Georgian suburb. In Victorian times its character changed to that of a poor and heavily populated district. Redevelopment since 1945 has been severe.

All these districts are represented in this book by photographs which were taken largely between 1890 and 1945. Though they are relatively recent in history, they show parts of London whose social, architectural and economic characters have changed so considerably that they seem different worlds today.

SOUTHWARK CATHEDRAL AND LONDON BRIDGE STATION

A hansom cab outside London Bridge Station.

St. Saviour's Parish Church became Southwark Cathedral in 1905. This view, of its south side, dates from a few years later. The nave (left of the tower) had been rebuilt by Sir Arthur Blomfield between 1890 and 1897.

The east end of Southwark Cathedral from the approach to London Bridge, *c.* 1910. The large gable beneath the tower surmounts the 13th-century choir and the four lower gables in front of it belong to the mediaeval retrochoir.

St. Saviour's Parish Church in 1885.

The unveiling of St. Saviour's War
Memorial in Borough High Street by
General Lord Horne, November 16th,
1922. The sculptor was P. Lindsay
Clark.

Cure's College in Park Street, Southwark, *c.* 1862. This was the principal set of almshouses for St. Saviour's Parish, later rebuilt at West Norwood when the railway displaced them.

The junction of Stoney Street and Southwark Street, *c.* 1910, roughly where Cure's College once stood. The Southwark Tavern on the left was one of the first buildings in Southwark Street. The Borough Market dominates this area.

Southwark Bridge Road District Library, July 5th, 1912, formerly the St. Saviour's Public Library.

The reading room of Southwark Bridge Road District Library, 1921.

London Bridge Station, *c.* 1860. The station forecourt is to the right and Duke Street Hill is to the left. Soon afterwards a viaduct was built to carry the line westwards to Charing Cross.

St. Thomas's Hospital and London Bridge Station, 1862. The hospital's ward blocks of 1840 are in the foreground. The lower buildings in the centre are 18th-century. The station is top left; the taller, turreted building to its right is the Terminus Hotel.

A hansom cab belonging to Thomas Tilling outside London Bridge Station, 1887.

London Bridge Station, *c.* 1931.

IN AND AROUND BOROUGH HIGH STREET

Private and public transport in Borough High Street.

Borough High Street, *c.* 1926, showing that era's characteristic mixture of motor and horse-drawn vehicles.

Borough High Street, 1881. The alley to the left of the figure was Brent's Court. Henry Dixon took this photograph and those on pages 24, 26, 27 and 33 for the Society for Photographing Relics of Old London, which was founded in 1875 to record buildings under threat of demolition. The pictures were printed in permanent carbon.

Newcomen Street, off Borough High Street, *c.* 1930. The yard to the right leads to hop warehouses, once characteristic of the area. The public house which juts out in the centre, the King's Arms, has the arms which adorned Old London Bridge.

Borough High Street, showing the entrance to Dun Horse Yard, 1910. This is just north of the junction with Marshalsea Road. The London & South Western Railway probably used the yard for minor storage purposes.

The front of the Marshalsea Prison, Borough High Street, 1832. The house set back from the rest (No. 150) was the Keeper's house. John Dickens spent three months here in 1824. (Guildhall Library, Corporation of London)

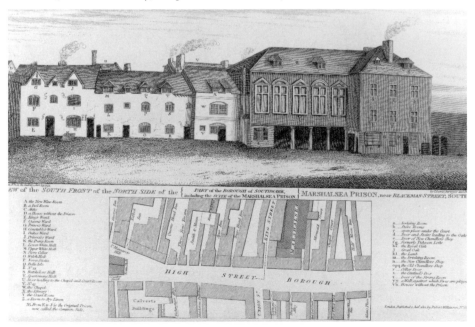

The Marshalsea Prison on its previous site in Borough High Street, 1773. The grander part on the right was the 17th-century court-house.

Children of Orange Street School, 1924.

Part of the London Fire Brigade's headquarters, Southwark Bridge Road, 1931, photographed by J. Dixon-Scott. The building on the right dates from 1878, when the famous Captain Shaw was in charge. The headquarters of the brigade moved to the Albert Embankment in the late 1930s. The building on the left is now an ordinary fire station, and the one on the right is part of the brigade's training establishment.

Redcross Cottages, built for Octavia Hill in the 1880s and seen here in about 1935. She had wanted to supersede the pattern of slum courts and tenement blocks.

Children from the poor streets near Long Lane, *c.* 1890. (Charterhouse-in-Southwark)

Mothers and children in a court near Long Lane, *c.* 1890. This photograph, and the one on the previous page, come from a large collection of views which were taken for the Charterhouse Mission a few years after its foundation in 1885. (Charterhouse-in-Southwark)

INNS OF BOROUGH HIGH STREET

A delivery cart in Borough High Street.

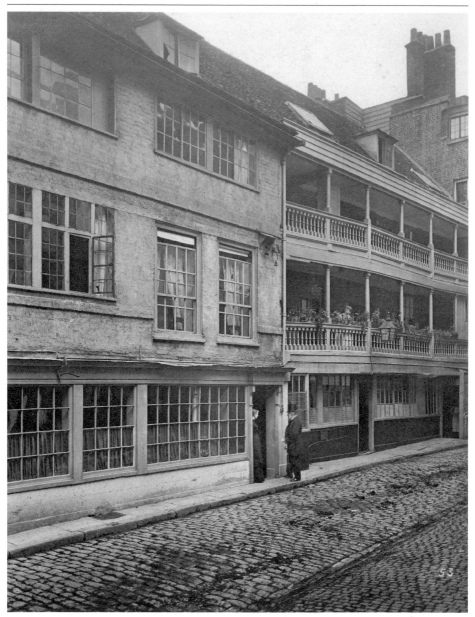

The George Inn, 1881, photographed by Henry Dixon. All the traditional coaching inns had a large yard for wagons, stables for horses, and bedrooms reached from open galleries.

The George Inn, *c.* 1920. At that time it still served as a hotel. These buildings are the only parts of any Southwark inn to remain.

The Tabard Inn, *c.* 1870. Chaucer made this inn the starting-point for his Canterbury pilgrims.

The Queen's Head Inn, 1881, photographed by Henry Dixon. In the 17th century this inn had been owned by John Harvard.

The White Hart Inn, 1882, from an engraving by Percy Thomas. This building, which was demolished in 1889, was where Charles Dickens set the momentous meeting between Mr Pickwick and Sam Weller.

The same scene as the above, but photographed by Henry Dixon, 1881.

A production of *As You Like It* in the yard of the George Inn, May 19th, 1956. Shakespeare's Globe Theatre stood about a quarter of a mile away.

BANKSIDE AND THE SOUTHWARK RIVERFRONT

Part of St. Mary Overy's Dock.

The widening of Blackfriars Bridge, 1908, seen from the Southwark side.

A sailing barge, seen in King's Reach (looking downstream).

Southwark Bridge, 1836. This was built by John Rennie between 1816 and 1819 and was the 'Iron Bridge' of Dickens's *Little Dorrit*.

An aerial view of London Bridge, facing Southwark, 1921. Note the great number of barges moored off Hay's Wharf on the left.

Old London Bridge, 1798. One of the alcoves seen along the parapet survives in the grounds of Guy's Hospital.

London Bridge looking towards the City, *c*. 1900. The view is taken roughly from Nancy's Steps in Southwark, a well-known setting in *Oliver Twist*.

St. Mary Overy's Dock, 1881, photographed by Henry Dixon. This dock was mentioned in Domesday Book in 1086.

Park Street, 1910, showing the arch which carries Southwark Bridge Road. Shakespeare's Globe Theatre stood just beyond the arch to the right.

The Tooley Street Fire of 1861, in which James Braidwood, Superintendent of the Metropolitan Fire Engine Establishment, was killed. St. Olave's Church stands to the right.

AROUND
BLACKFRIARS
ROAD

The Surrey Theatre in Blackfriars Road.

An aerial view of the river at Blackfriars Bridge, 1920. Christ Church, in Blackfriars Road, is in the bottom right-hand corner.

Hopton's Almshouses, 1900. These 18th-century buildings survive in Hopton Street, off Southwark Street.

Weatherboarded houses in Collingwood Street, off Blackfriars Road, *c.* 1920.

The removal of human remains from the crypt of Christ Church, Blackfriars Road, April 23rd, 1895. Christ Church was extensively restored and extended in the 1890s. The clearing of burials from the crypt was one part of that process. It was quite common in the 1890s for the crypts of 17th- and 18th-century churches to be cleared of buried remains, which were then taken to various cemeteries in and around London. The remains in this case went out to Brookwood Cemetery near Woking.

St. George's Circus, 1812, showing the Surrey Theatre in the background, to the left, and, in front of it, the tollgate at the start of Blackfriars Road. On the extreme left is the obelisk which is now in the grounds of the Imperial War Museum.

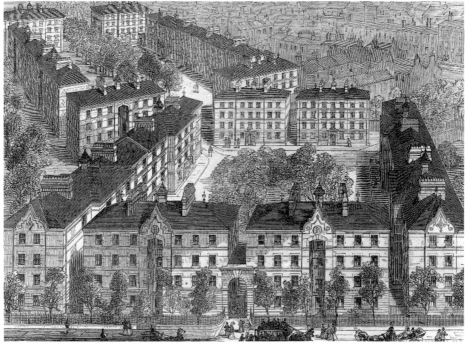

Peabody Square, Blackfriars Road, *c.* 1872. Tenement blocks were built in Southwark in large numbers from the 1870s to the First World War.

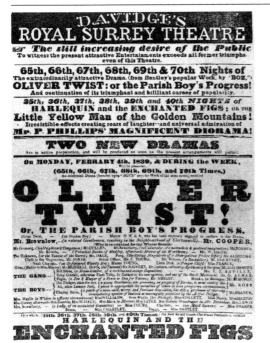

A Surrey Theatre playbill dating from early in Dickens's career, 1839.

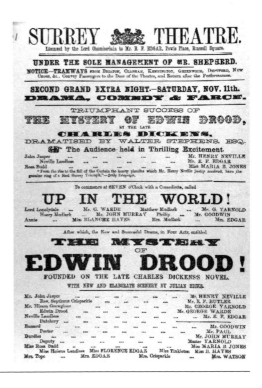

And one from after his death in 1870.

Surrey Chapel stood at the corner of Blackfriars Road and Union Street. It was built between 1782 and 1783 for Rowland Hill (top left) and closed as a chapel in 1881. At the time of its closure the minister was Benjamin Senior (right). The building was put to commercial use and later housed a boxing ring (see below). It was destroyed in 1940.

The Ring between the wars. For most of that period the property was run by Bella Burge.

THE PARISH OF
ST. GEORGE
THE MARTYR

St. George the Martyr Church, 1814.

Borough High Street in 1931, looking towards St. George the Martyr Church (the 'Little Dorrit church'). The other apparent spire was a ventilation tower in Guy's Hospital.

Employees of the Vestry of St. George the Martyr, Southwark, at the Swan Street Depot, *c.* 1891. Most of the men were street sweepers. The man on the right was the horse keeper.

A watercolour of Lant Street, off Borough High Street, by J.P. Emslie, 1898. The house to the left of the archway belonged to the Vestry Clerk of St. George the Martyr when Charles Dickens lodged there in 1824.

The Mint Street Workhouse, *c.* 1920, originally the workhouse for St. George's Parish. The original caption refers to it as St. George's Institution.

An early Boots store in London Road, February 14th, 1904, photographed by Ernest Milner.

The Bridge House Public House, Borough Road, 1897. It is named after the estate which forms the endowment of the City of London's four Thames bridges.

Borough Road Baptist Chapel at the turn of the century.

A group outside Borough Road Baptist Chapel in 1931.

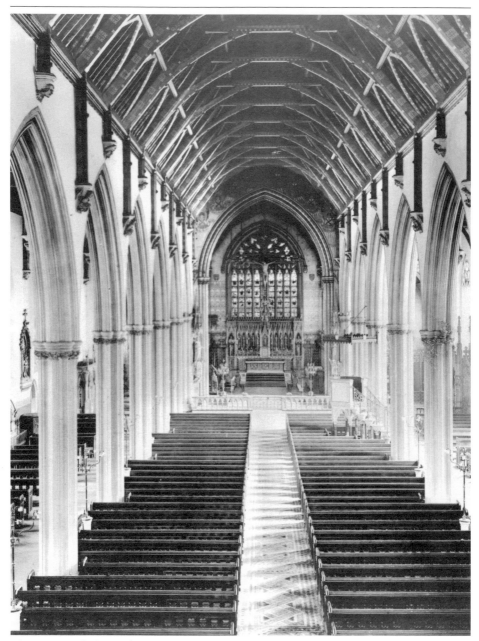

The nave and choir of St. George's Cathedral, 1923, photographed by J. Dixon-Scott. The architect was A.W.N. Pugin and the building was erected between 1840 and 1848. It became the cathedral of the new Roman Catholic Diocese of Southwark in 1850.

THE ELEPHANT
AND CASTLE

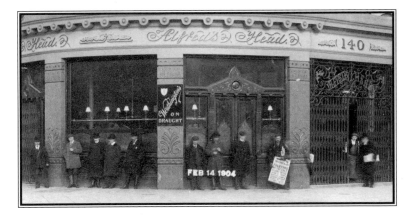

Outside the Alfred's Head Public House.

A postcard of the Elephant and Castle in 1907. The public house (right) from which the place takes its name had been rebuilt in 1898. New Kent Road runs off to the left and Walworth Road is in the centre. The sign of the Elephant and Castle can be seen between the two smaller domes on the roof of the public house. The sign's use on this site was first recorded in 1765.

The Alfred's Head Public House at the Elephant and Castle, February 14th, 1904.

Newington Butts in 1930. The public house in the middle of the view is the Alfred's Head; the road receding into the distance to its right is Newington Causeway.

Walworth Road, 1930. The Elephant and Castle Public House is the grand building in the centre background.

The Elephant and Castle from Walworth Road in 1898. The famous public house was to be rebuilt that year. Note the man digging out the groove of the tramline.

Newington Causeway from the Elephant and Castle junction, *c.* 1907. The Rockingham Arms is on the right. The large store to the left of it was Risdon, Locke & Co., formerly Tarn's the draper. The electric tram on the left is leaving Walworth Road for Blackfriars.

The Elephant and Castle Theatre, New Kent Road, *c.* 1907.

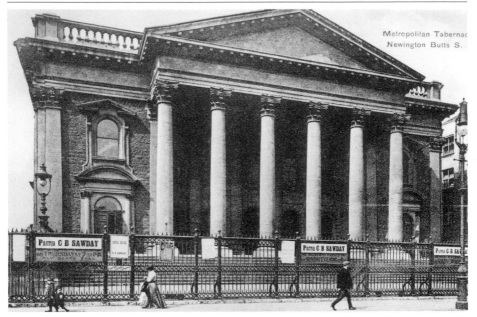

The Metropolitan Tabernacle, Newington Butts, 1905. This huge Baptist church was first built for C.H. Spurgeon between 1859 and 1861 and could hold nearly 5,000 people. It was rebuilt on a smaller scale after a fire in 1898.

Charles Haddon Spurgeon (1834–1892), 'the prince of preachers'.

THE PARISH OF ST. MARY, NEWINGTON

Pupils of St. Mary's Girls' School.

St. Mary's Church,
Newington Butts, *c.* 1864.

St. Mary's in 1866. This building
dated from 1792 and was designed
by Francis Hurlbatt. It was replaced
on a site in Kennington Park Road
in 1876 (see page 56).

Newington Butts, looking north, *c.* 1870. St. Mary's Church is in the background.

The Rectory of St. Mary's, *c.* 1870. This very old house had substantial grounds and had once been moated.

St. Mary's Church in Kennington Park Road, *c.* 1892. The church was built in 1876 as the successor to the one on page 54. The architect was James Fowler.

Newington Clock Tower, 1889. It had been erected in the old churchyard of St. Mary's, Newington, in 1877.

The entrance to St. Mary's Schools, June 25th, 1897.

Room G, St. Mary's Girls' School, April 1911. This school stood on the site of the baths at the Elephant and Castle.

A presentation of Christmas gifts to pensioners on behalf of the charities of St. Mary, Newington, 1930. The ancient parishes became the administrators of many charities between Tudor and Victorian times, and boards of trustees have continued to administer them in the 20th century.

WALWORTH AND THE OLD KENT ROAD

Feeding the animals at the Surrey Zoological Gardens.

Walworth Manor House, *c.* 1865. The house stood at the junction of Manor Place and Penton Place and had been built for Thomas Clutton in 1786. From 1862 to 1871 it was part of St. Thomas's Hospital. The grounds attached to the house served as the Surrey Gardens between 1831 and 1878, comprising at different times a zoo (see opposite), a music hall, and a setting for firework displays, ascents by hot-air balloon and various public spectacles.

Giraffes in the Surrey Zoological Gardens, which occupied the grounds of Walworth Manor House, 1843. There is still a Giraffe Public House in Penton Place. The zoological gardens were set up in 1831 by Edward Cross, who had previously kept a menagerie in the Strand. The animals were removed in 1855.

A horse parade outside the baths and wash-houses in Manor Place, Walworth, 1912.
The baths were in use from 1898 to 1978. They were built for the Vestry of the Parish
of St. Mary, Newington, and passed into the hands of the Metropolitan Borough of
Southwark in 1900. Local authorities possessed many horses in the 19th and early 20th
centuries, and parades were held annually.

An Edwardian postcard of East Street Market, with the Rising Sun Public House in the background.

George Thomas Rhodes's 'Lamp Hospital' at 323 East Street, Walworth, *c.* 1900.

The Paragon, New Kent Road, *c.* 1890. This crescent, designed by Michael Searles, was built for John Rolls between 1787 and 1788. Incredibly, it was demolished to make way for a board school at the turn of this century.

The reference section of Southwark Central Library, Walworth Road, 1921. Note the decorative panel by George Tinworth above the catalogue to the right.

Children at Flint Street School, Walworth, early 20th century.

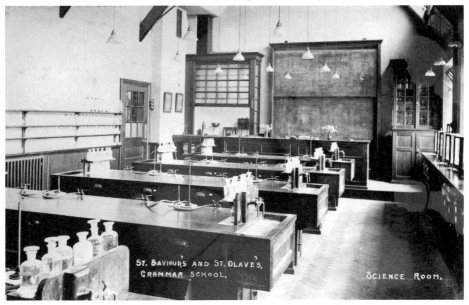

The Science Room of St. Saviour's and St. Olave's Grammar School for Girls, New Kent Road, 1925.

A tram in Old Kent Road just before its withdrawal from service, 1952.

The Georgian premises of John Edgington & Co. Ltd, in the Old Kent Road, 1967. These were swept away for the megalomaniac flyover scheme in 1969.

Section Ten

BERMONDSEY

Women enjoying a club outing in Bermondsey.

The interior of the church of the Most Holy Trinity, Dockhead, *c.* 1919. The church was built from 1834 to 1835 by J.J. Scoles and was bombed in 1940.

Women's club outing photographed in front of the Old Margate Town Public House, George Row, *c.* 1930.

Crosse and Blackwell's factory in Crimscott Street: one of the area's many food-processing plants, *c.* 1930. The lack of space for expansion and difficulties over access for large lorries were important factors in the eventual removal of such factories from the area.

The staff of East Lane School, *c*. 1900. The headmaster, Mr. W.G. Smith, is in the centre at the front.

The Star Cinema, Abbey Street, 1937. This view shows the 'tuppenny rush'.

Children at Monarch Buildings, Bermondsey, *c.* 1920. (Mrs. J. Warren)

Southwark Park Road, *c.* 1928. This was Bermondsey's high street.

Spa Road, the location of many civic buildings, *c.* 1906. The baths stand to the right; the tall building in the centre with a flagpole is the town hall; and the turreted building beyond is the library.

Bermondsey Central Baths in Grange Road, *c.* 1930. These baths replaced the ones in Spa Road (in the picture above). They were in use until 1975.

Police removing a barricade erected in Long Lane to block Oswald Mosley's marchers, October 3rd, 1937.

Delivering the milk in Southwark Park Road, January 1940.

Bricklayers' Arms Station, 1863. Then a passenger terminus, later it was a goods depot only.

Tower Bridge, *c.* 1900. It had been opened in 1894 and became an important route to and from Bermondsey. The barges are lying off Courage's Brewery at Horselydown.

HOUSING IN BERMONDSEY AND ROTHERHITHE

Residents of Neckinger Place.

Balin Place, off Long Lane, typical of so many alleys and courts in prewar Bermondsey. Note the external shutters on the ground-floor windows: they were once ubiquitous in the area.

Wilderness Street, 1934. More shutters may be seen.

Cherry Garden Street, Bermondsey, 1934. The name of the side-street, Cranbourne Place, recalls the area's ancient ownership by the Earls of Salisbury, who were also Viscounts Cranbourne.

Sard's Rents in the shadow of the railway viaduct over Tower Bridge Road, *c.* 1937.

Arnold's Place, looking towards Tooley Street, January 1936. Note the ground-floor shutters and the advertisement (on the left) for the *Bermondsey Labour Magazine*.

Jacob Street, Dockhead, *c.* 1920. This was the road which ran across 'Jacob's Island', the slum depicted in *Oliver Twist*.

A mid-Victorian drawing of Jacob's Island. The waterways which made it an island were connected to the watermill next to St. Saviour's Dock.

Children outside some houses in Rotherhithe Street, 1929.

An eviction scene in a Bermondsey court, *c.* 1896, used for propaganda purposes in *Bermondsey Parish Church Reports*. Bermondsey Parish Church was engaged in a vigorous campaign towards the end of the last century to show the world how dreadful were the conditions in Bermondsey and how much the parish was doing to combat them. No doubt fund-raising was involved, but ultimately the plan was one of evangelization.

Neckinger Place, January 1936.

Wolseley Buildings from George Row, 1936. These tenements, built in 1883, are typical of the late Victorian period.

Abbey Buildings at the junction of Tower Bridge Road and Abbey Street, 1976. They were subsequently demolished. They had been built by a railway company on part of the site of the mediaeval Bermondsey Abbey. (Mr C. Rumbold).

Neckinger Estate, 1938: a block of Bermondsey Borough Council's flats when new.

Bermondsey Borough Council's new cottages in Albion Street, Rotherhithe, 1931. These were naturally much more popular than the contemporary tenement blocks.

Acorn Walk at Rotherhithe, 1931.

Bermondsey Borough Council's flats in West Lane, 1935.

Nos. 101–107 Weston Street, Bermondsey, 1959. No. 103 (in whose doorway the man is standing) had once been known as 3 Minver Place and was where Frederick and Maria Manning murdered their lodger in 1849. They were publicly hanged outside Horsemonger Lane Prison. The case was one of the most notorious in Victorian London.

MUNICIPAL

BERMONDSEY

Blacksmiths at work.

A meeting of Bermondsey Borough Council in the session of 1902–3. Above the Mayor (Alexander Burton) are the borough's arms, showing a lion with a crozier (for Bermondsey Abbey), a crown and an axe (for St. Olave's) and a ship (for Rotherhithe). The borough existed from 1900 to 1965. Its first mayor was Colonel S.B. Bevington, the head of the foremost local leather firm.

Street cleaning in Alma Grove in 1936. Many people would revive the Borough of Bermondsey today if they could do so.

A Bermondsey Borough Council sewerman, 1936.

Alfred Salter, Doctor of Medicine and Member of Parliament for West Bermondsey, seen here in 1932. He was a noted crusader to improve living conditions in Bermondsey and is still fondly remembered today. He died in 1945.

Ada Salter, a notable member of Bermondsey Borough Council and of the London County Council. She was Alfred Salter's wife.

Dr. Alfred Salter plants a tree during the opening ceremony of Tanner Street Recreation
Ground in May 1929. Councillor George Horwood, the Mayor of Bermondsey, stands
on the right. Ben Smith, M.P. for Rotherhithe from 1923 to 1931 and 1935 to 1946,
stands between the mayor and Alfred Salter. The woman holding a shovel is Councillor
Mrs. Ada Salter, Alfred's wife, who was the Chairman of the Beautification Committee
of Bermondsey Borough Council. The clergyman behind her is Alderman the Reverend
Andrew Amos, Rector of Rotherhithe.

Bermondsey Borough Council's General Purposes Committee, 1930. The mayor is Councillor A.C. Starr. To his left is Andrew Amos, Rector of Rotherhithe and an alderman of the borough.

Bermondsey Borough Council's blacksmith's shop, 1937.

LEATHER MANUFACTURING IN BERMONDSEY

Finishing skivers and persians at Neckinger

Leather Mills.

Messrs. Bevingtons & Sons' Neckinger Leather Mills, seen from Neckinger, 1931.

Lime pits at Neckinger Leather Mills, 1931. A huge number of such pits once featured on the map of Bermondsey.

Breaking, unhairing and fleshing sheepskins at the Mills, 1862. Note that the men are using two-handled knives to scrape the skins. Unhairing was the process of scraping away the hair of the animal and fleshing was the removal of small bits of flesh adhering to the inner surface of the skins.

Finishing skivers and persians for hat linings and boot leather at the Mills, 1862. Note the election poster on the left. (The candidate was Sir Austen Henry Layard (1817–1894), who is now perhaps best known as the archaeologist who discovered Nineveh, the ancient capital of the Assyrian Empire.)

Conditioning skins at the Mills, 1931. This part of the works was under the railway arches.

The London Leather Exchange, Weston Street, c. 1879.

The staff of the leather manufacturing firm of George Whichelow, probably at the turn of the century.

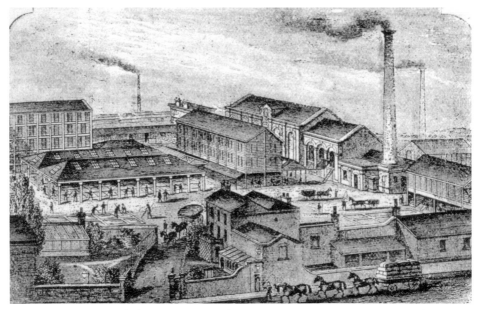

The Grange Tannery, belonging to Samuel Barrow & Bros., 1876.

Section Fourteen

ROTHERHITHE

The Angel Public House.

Rotherhithe Street between Fulford Street and Cathay Street, 1937. The Angel Public House is at the far end of the block on the right.

Elephant Lane, 1937. It was typical of the ancient, narrow streets in the old part of the district.

The Angel Public House at Rotherhithe Stairs, early this century. The Angel is the oldest known tavern name in the area. The houses to the left were destroyed in the Second World War. The premises of Messrs. Willmott and Cobon, on the right, occupied the site of King Edward III's 14th-century manor-house, which has been excavated in recent years.

An Edwardian postcard of Lower Road, showing Southwark Park Wesleyan Methodist Church in the centre and St. Mary's School to the left.

Rotherhithe Free Church, Lower Road, *c*. 1905. It was rebuilt shortly afterwards for its pastor, Thomas Richardson, who was an independent evangelist. He succeeded in drawing huge congregations to his services in Lower Road, and the construction of what he called the Rotherhithe Great Hall was a conspicuous mark of his success.

Paradise Street in December, 1938. 'Paradise' was an old name for an enclosed garden. The street name may derive from a property whose existence was recorded in 1631, and which probably had a large, enclosed garden.

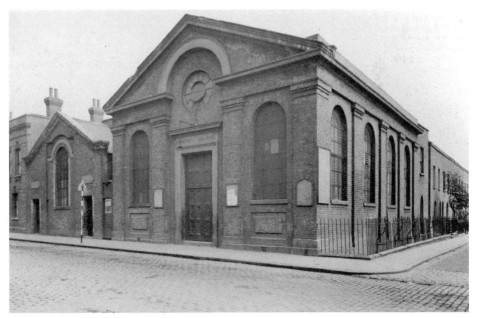

Albion Street United Methodist Chapel. This had been built in 1852 by seceders from the Wesleyan Methodists.

A group of clergy and lay officials outside St. Mary's Church, Rotherhithe, *c.* 1900. Canon Edward Beck, Rector from 1867 to 1907, stands in the centre. In 1907 he wrote the only full-scale book on Rotherhithe's history so far published.

All Saints' Church, Lower Road, 1938. The church was destroyed in the Second World War.

By the boating lake in Southwark Park in Edwardian days.

Flooding outside Lavender House, Rotherhithe Street, February 2nd, 1953.

Rotherhithe Street, at the junction with Silver Street, 1932.

Noah's Ark Public House, Rotherhithe Street, *c.* 1930. The alley on the right was once called Screw Post Row.

THE SURREY DOCKS AND THE ROTHERHITHE RIVERFRONT

A horse-drawn wagon at the Surrey Docks.

The main entrance to the Surrey Docks, Lower Road, 1907.

A characteristic view of the dominant timber trade in the Docks, probably in about 1910. The timber came from the Baltic and Canada, hence Canada Dock, Quebec Pond, Norway Dock, etc.

Station Yard at the Docks, 1907. Note the sign for the Swedish Seamen's Church above the man on the far left.

Transporting paper from the Docks in horse-drawn wagons, 1922.

Greenland Dock, *c.* 1925. Note that the ships are surrounded by barges: a characteristic practice of the Port of London. This came about because of the long-standing influence of the lightermen. When the enclosed wet docks were formed, at the very end of the 18th century, pressure from the lightermen led to the insertion into the Acts for building the docks of the so-called 'free-water clause', by which lighters (or barges) could enter the docks without charge. Many ships in the Port of London were therefore unloaded into barges, for removal of the goods to warehouses upstream, rather than on to the quays of the docks themselves.

Greenland Dock, seen from the swing bridge in Redriff Road, 1960.

Lower Road, *c.* 1908, with Station Yard in Surrey Commercial Docks on the left and Deptford Road Station (renamed Surrey Docks Station in 1911) on the right.

An iron church at Rotherhithe, *c.* 1903, which served the Finnish community. The Surrey Commercial Docks transacted much business with the Baltic countries.

The Thames at Rotherhithe in Georgian times, showing St. Mary's Church.

The diving bell was used during an irruption of water in the Thames Tunnel, May 18th, 1827. St. Mary's Church, Rotherhithe, is in the background on the right.

River scene near the Angel Public House, *c.* 1914.

The Lower Pool in 1930, looking upstream. Most of the warehouses on the left were used as granaries.

The tug, the *John Wilson*, at Point Wharf, Rotherhithe. It was built for the firm of Humphery and Grey.

The Surrey Docks in 1934, looking eastwards, with Limehouse Reach towards the top. Note the innumerable timber sheds.

THE SECOND

WORLD WAR

A Victory party in Long Lane.

Bomb damage in Lower Road, Rotherhithe, 1940. The Methodist Church is to the left. A view across the cleared site is on the opposite page.

Bomb damage in Neptune Street, Rotherhithe, September 1940.

Lower Road, Rotherhithe in July 1950. St. Mary's School is on the left and the bombed Methodist Church is on the right.

The Rotherhithe Hippodrome (originally Terriss's Theatre), Lower Road, 1954.

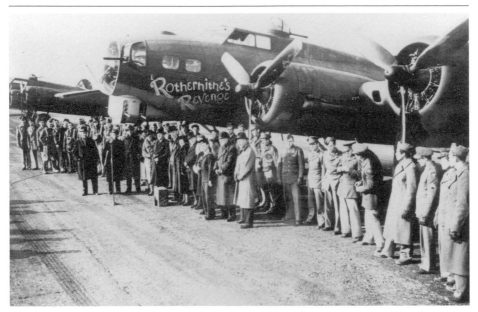

'Rotherhithe's Revenge', 1943. People were encouraged to buy Savings Certificates, to be cashed in after the war, and money raised went towards 'buying' this Boeing Flying Fortress. As a reward, the US authorities allowed it to be named after the borough, which had suffered badly in the Blitz.

The Surrey Docks in the Blitz, September 1940.

Bermondsey Women's Voluntary Service, 1944.

A bread queue in Spa Road, Bermondsey, 1946. Rationing continued for some years after the war.

King George VI and Queen Elizabeth (the present Queen Mother) outside an air-raid shelter in Brunel Road, Rotherhithe, in 1941. The visit took place at the height of the Blitz, in which the Surrey Docks suffered severely.

A Victory party outside the Ship Public House, Long Lane, Bermondsey, 1945.

A Victory party on the Kirby Estate, Rotherhithe, May 1945.

A 'prefab' in Abbey Street, Bermondsey, 1946. Built as a temporary measure to ease the housing shortage, they became a long-lasting result of the Second World War.

The interior of the house above.

ROYAL OCCASIONS

The Coronation drive of King George V and

Queen Mary.

Newington Public Library (later Southwark Central Library), Walworth Road, decorated for Queen Victoria's Diamond Jubilee in 1897. The building to the left is the Newington Vestry Hall, built in 1866. The library had opened in 1893.

Fogden's, on the corner of Long Lane and Staple Street, Bermondsey, during the carnival of July 19th, 1900. This event was held to raise funds to relieve families affected by the Boer War.

The mayors of the South London boroughs present their addresses to King George V and Queen Mary outside Borough Road Library during his Coronation drive in 1911.

The Southwark contingent for a Festival of Empire Pageant waits outside Southwark Town Hall, Walworth Road, to see King George V and Queen Mary pass by on their way to the Crystal Palace, May 12th, 1911.

The opening ceremony of St. Saviour's and St. Olave's Grammar School for Girls, New Kent Road, March 14th, 1903, led by the Prince and Princess of Wales (later King George V and Queen Mary).

A children's party in Alscot Road, Bermondsey, 1935, to mark King George V's Silver Jubilee.

To order any of these titles please telephone Littlehampton Book Services on 01903 721596

Scunthorpe, *D Taylor*
Skegness, *W Kime*
Around Skegness, *W Kime*

LONDON

Balham and Tooting, *P Loobey*
Crystal Palace, Penge & Anerley, *M Scott*
Greenwich and Woolwich, *K Clark*
Hackney: A Second Selection, *D Mander*
Lewisham and Deptford, *J Coulter*
Lewisham and Deptford: A Second Selection, *J Coulter*
Streatham, *P Loobey*
Around Whetstone and North Finchley, *J Heathfield*
Woolwich, *B Evans*

MONMOUTHSHIRE

Chepstow and the River Wye, *A Rainsbury*
Monmouth and the River Wye, *Monmouth Museum*

NORFOLK

Great Yarmouth, *M Teun*
Norwich, *M Colman*
Wymondham and Attleborough, *P Yaxley*

NORTHAMPTONSHIRE

Around Stony Stratford, *A Lambert*

NOTTINGHAMSHIRE

Arnold and Bestwood, *M Spick*
Arnold and Bestwood: A Second Selection, *M Spick*
Changing Face of Nottingham, *G Oldfield*
Mansfield, *Old Mansfield Society*
Around Newark, *T Warner*
Nottingham: 1944–1974, *D Whitworth*
Sherwood Forest, *D Ottewell*
Victorian Nottingham, *M Payne*

OXFORDSHIRE

Around Abingdon, *P Horn*
Banburyshire, *M Barnett & S Gosling*
Burford, *A Jewell*
Around Didcot and the Hagbournes, *B Lingham*
Garsington, *M Gunther*
Around Henley-on-Thames, *S Ellis*
Oxford: The University, *J Rhodes*
Thame to Watlington, *N Hood*
Around Wallingford, *D Beasley*
Witney, *T Worley*
Around Witney, *C Mitchell*
Witney District, *T Worley*
Around Woodstock, *J Bond*

POWYS

Brecon, *Brecknock Museum*
Welshpool, *E Bredsdorff*

SHROPSHIRE

Shrewsbury, *D Trumper*
Whitchurch to Market Drayton, *M Morris*

SOMERSET

Bath, *J Hudson*
Bridgwater and the River Parrett, *R Fitzhugh*
Bristol, *D Moorcroft & N Campbell-Sharp*
Changing Face of Keynsham,
  B Lowe & M Whitehead

Chard and Ilminster, *G Gosling & F Huddy*
Crewkerne and the Ham Stone Villages,
  G Gosling & F Huddy
Around Keynsham and Saltford, *B Lowe & T Brown*
Midsomer Norton and Radstock, *C Howell*
Somerton, Ilchester and Langport, *G Gosling & F Huddy*
Taunton, *N Chipchase*
Around Taunton, *N Chipchase*
Wells, *C Howell*
Weston-Super-Mare, *S Poole*
Around Weston-Super-Mare, *S Poole*
West Somerset Villages, *K Houghton & L Thomas*

STAFFORDSHIRE

Aldridge, *J Farrow*
Bilston, *E Rees*
Black Country Transport: Aviation, *A Brew*
Around Burton upon Trent, *G Sowerby & R Farman*
Bushbury, *A Chatwin, M Mills & E Rees*
Around Cannock, *M Mills & S Belcher*
Around Leek, *R Poole*
Lichfield, *H Clayton & K Simmons*
Around Pattingham and Wombourne, *M Griffiths,*
  P Leigh & M Mills
Around Rugeley, *T Randall & J Anslow*
Smethwick, *J Maddison*
Stafford, *J Anslow & T Randall*
Around Stafford, *J Anslow & T Randall*
Stoke-on-Trent, *I Lawley*
Around Tamworth, *R Sulima*
Around Tettenhall and Codsall, *M Mills*
Tipton, Wednesbury and Darlaston, *R Pearson*
Walsall, *D Gilbert & M Lewis*
Wednesbury, *I Bott*
West Bromwich, *R Pearson*

SUFFOLK

Ipswich: A Second Selection, *D Kindred*
Around Ipswich, *D Kindred*
Around Mildenhall, *C Dring*
Southwold to Aldeburgh, *H Phelps*
Around Woodbridge, *H Phelps*

SURREY

Cheam and Belmont, *P Berry*
Croydon, *S Bligh*
Dorking and District, *K Harding*
Around Dorking, *A Jackson*
Around Epsom, *P Berry*
Farnham: A Second Selection, *J Parratt*
Around Haslemere and Hindhead, *T Winter & G Collyer*
Richmond, *Richmond Local History Society*
Sutton, *P Berry*

SUSSEX

Arundel and the Arun Valley, *J Godfrey*
Bishopstone and Seaford, *P Pople & P Berry*
Brighton and Hove, *J Middleton*
Brighton and Hove: A Second Selection, *J Middleton*
Around Crawley, *M Goldsmith*
Hastings, *P Haines*
Hastings: A Second Selection, *P Haines*
Around Haywards Heath, *J Middleton*
Around Heathfield, *A Gillet & B Russell*
Around Heathfield: A Second Selection,
  A Gillet & B Russell
High Weald, *B Harwood*
High Weald: A Second Selection, *B Harwood*
Horsham and District, *T Wales*

Lewes, *J Middleton*
RAF Tangmere, *A Saunders*
Around Rye, *A Dickinson*
Around Worthing, *S White*

WARWICKSHIRE

Along the Avon from Stratford to Tewkesbury, *J Jeremiah*
Bedworth, *J Burton*
Coventry, *D McGrory*
Around Coventry, *D McGrory*
Nuneaton, *S Clews & S Vaughan*
Around Royal Leamington Spa, *J Cameron*
Around Royal Leamington Spa: A Second Selection,
  J Cameron
Around Warwick, *R Booth*

WESTMORLAND

Eden Valley, *J Marsh*
Kendal, *M & P Duff*
South Westmorland Villages, *J Marsh*
Westmorland Lakes, *J Marsh*

WILTSHIRE

Around Amesbury, *P Daniels*
Chippenham and Lacock, *A Wilson & M Wilson*
Around Corsham and Box, *A Wilson & M Wilson*
Around Devizes, *D Buxton*
Around Highworth, *G Tanner*
Around Highworth and Faringdon, *G Tanner*
Around Malmesbury, *A Wilson*
Marlborough: A Second Selection, *P Colman*
Around Melksham,
  Melksham and District Historical Association
Nadder Valley, *R. Sawyer*
Salisbury, *P Saunders*
Salisbury: A Second Selection, *P Daniels*
Salisbury: A Third Selection, *P Daniels*
Around Salisbury, *P Daniels*
Swindon: A Third Selection, *The Swindon Society*
Swindon: A Fourth Selection, *The Swindon Society*
Trowbridge, *M Marshman*
Around Wilton, *P Daniels*
Around Wootton Bassett, Cricklade and Purton, *T Sharp*

WORCESTERSHIRE

Evesham to Bredon, *F Archer*
Around Malvern, *K Smith*
Around Pershore, *M Dowty*
Redditch and the Needle District, *R Saunders*
Redditch: A Second Selection, *R Saunders*
Around Tenbury Wells, *D Green*
Worcester, *M Dowty*
Around Worcester, *R Jones*
Worcester in a Day, *M Dowty*
Worcestershire at Work, *R Jones*

YORKSHIRE

Huddersfield: A Second Selection, *H Wheeler*
Huddersfield: A Third Selection, *H Wheeler*
Leeds Road and Rail, *R Vickers*
Pontefract, *R van Riel*
Scarborough, *D Coggins*
Scarborough's War Years, *R Percy*
Skipton and the Dales, *Friends of the Craven Museum*
Around Skipton-in-Craven, *Friends of the Craven Museum*
Yorkshire Wolds, *I & M Sumner*